56 Fertility Increasing Juice Recipes:

Juice Your Way to Higher Fertility Levels through Natures Ingredients

By

Joe Correa CSN

COPYRIGHT

© 2018 Live Stronger Faster Inc.

All rights reserved

Reproduction or translation of any part of this work beyond that permitted by section 107 or 108 of the 1976 United States Copyright Act without the permission of the copyright owner is unlawful.

This publication is designed to provide accurate and authoritative information in regard to the subject matter covered. It is sold with the understanding that neither the author nor the publisher is engaged in rendering medical advice. If medical advice or assistance is needed, consult with a doctor. This book is considered a guide and should not be used in any way detrimental to your health. Consult with a physician before starting this nutritional plan to make sure it's right for you.

ACKNOWLEDGEMENTS

This book is dedicated to my friends and family that have had mild or serious illnesses so that you may find a solution and make the necessary changes in your life.

56 Fertility Increasing Juice Recipes:

Juice Your Way to Higher Fertility Levels through Natures Ingredients

By

Joe Correa CSN

CONTENTS

Copyright

Acknowledgements

About The Author

Introduction

Commitment

56 Fertility Increasing Juice Recipes: Juice Your Way to Higher Fertility Levels through Natures Ingredients

Additional Titles from This Author

ABOUT THE AUTHOR

After years of Research, I honestly believe in the positive effects that proper nutrition can have over the body and mind. My knowledge and experience has helped me live healthier throughout the years and which I have shared with family and friends. The more you know about eating and drinking healthier, the sooner you will want to change your life and eating habits.

Nutrition is a key part in the process of being healthy and living longer so get started today. The first step is the most important and the most significant.

INTRODUCTION

56 Fertility Increasing Juice Recipes: Juice Your Way to Higher Fertility Levels through Natures Ingredients

By Joe Correa CSN

About 15% of couples are affected by some form of fertility issue. Sadly most couples struggle for years with this problem and it affects their relationship, their mental health, and overall life. Unknowingly, they repeat some bad habits which affect their fertility every single day.

Luckily, unless you're having some serious medical problems, there are some easy ways and steps to help you improve your overall fertility. All doctors agree that lifestyle and diet affect fertility up to 69%. This huge percentage can easily become reality by adopting some good habits and small changes that will do wonders for your body and your sexual health.

There are some natural and healthy ways which are proven to help improve fertility:

1. Start your day with a big breakfast! Not only will eating a proper breakfast help you boost your energy levels, it will also improve the hormonal balance you need in order to improve fertility.

2. Choose foods rich in antioxidants! Antioxidants are known to deactivate free radicals in your body which directly preserves both sperm and egg cells.
3. Reduce carbs, especially refined ones! A low carb diet is often recommended as a part of the treatment for women with polycystic ovaries. Furthermore, this type of diet will help you reduce weight and reduce insulin levels which will in return help menstrual regularity.
4. Eat more fiber in the form of fruits, vegetables, and whole grains. Some types of fiber help remove excess estrogen from the body which leads to improved sexual health.
5. Get active and take time to relax! These two important life habits are proven to help you resolve not only sexual problems but many other health issues you might be having. So take the time to get active and do the things you enjoy!

Once you have adopted these easy and healthy lifestyle habits, you will notice some positive changes in your body which will come as a result of hormonal balance and good sexual health. As I said earlier, consuming the right foods is probably the most important thing you can do to improve your fertility.

For this reason, I have created a delicious collection of 56 juice recipes that will help you improve your fertility levels quickly and naturally. These recipes are high in fiber, antioxidants, and other important nutrients your body needs to heal itself. They are perfectly healthy, mind-blowing delicious, and designed especially for you! Give them a try!

56 FERTILITY INCREASING JUICE RECIPES

1. **Spinach Blackberry Juice**

Ingredients:

1 cup fresh spinach, torn

1 cup blackberries

1 cup mango, chunked

3 whole apricots, chopped

1 whole lime, peeled

Preparation:

Rinse the spinach thoroughly under cold running water. Drain and torn into small pieces. Set aside.

Rinse the blackberries using a large colander. Drain and set aside.

Peel the mango and cut into small chunks. Fill the measuring cup and reserve the rest for later. Set aside.

Wash the apricots and cut in half. Remove the pits and chop into small pieces. Set aside.

Peel the lime and cut lengthwise in half. Set aside.

Now, combine spinach, blackberries, mango, apricots, and lime in a juicer. Process until juiced. Transfer to a serving glass and refrigerate for 10 minutes before serving.

Enjoy!

Nutrition information per serving: Kcal: 201, Protein: 11.1g, Carbs: 61.5g, Fats: 2.6g

2. Sweet Apple Ginger Juice

Ingredients:

1 large Granny Smith's apple, cored and chopped

1 small ginger knob, peeled

1 cup celery, chopped

1 cup fresh mint, torn

1 tsp liquid honey

1 oz water

Preparation:

Wash the apple and cut lengthwise in half. Remove the core and cut into bite-sized pieces. Set aside.

Peel the ginger knob and chop into small pieces. Set aside.

Wash the celery and chop into small pieces. Fill the measuring cup and reserve the rest for later.

Rinse the mint thoroughly under cold running water. Drain and torn into small pieces.

Now, combine apple, ginger, celery, and mint in a juicer and process until well juiced. Transfer to a serving glass and stir in the honey and water.

Refrigerate for 15 minutes before serving.

Enjoy!

Nutrition information per serving: Kcal: 121, Protein: 2.6g, Carbs: 35.8g, Fats: 0.8g

3. Pumpkin Pomegranate Juice

Ingredients:

1 cup yellow pumpkin, cubed

1 cup pomegranate seeds

3 whole plums, pitted and chopped

1 medium-sized orange, peeled

¼ tsp ginger, ground

1 oz water

Preparation:

Cut the top of a pumpkin. Cut lengthwise in half and then scrape out the seeds. Cut one large wedge and peel it. Cut into small cubes and fill the measuring cup. Reserve the rest in the refrigerator.

Cut the top of the pomegranate fruit using a sharp paring knife. Slice down to each of the white membranes inside of the fruit. Pop the seeds into a measuring cup and set aside.

Wash the plums and cut into halves. Remove the pits and chop into small pieces. Set aside.

Peel the orange and divide into wedges. Cut each wedge

in half and set aside.

Now, combine pumpkin, pomegranate, plums, and orange in a juicer. Process until juiced. Transfer to a serving glass and stir in the ginger and water.

Refrigerate for 10 minutes before serving.

Enjoy!

Nutrition information per serving: Kcal: 214, Protein: 5.2g, Carbs: 61.8g, Fats: 1.8g

4. Blueberry Grapefruit Juice

Ingredients:

1 cup blueberries

1 whole grapefruit, peeled

1 cup avocado, cubed

1 small Red Delicious apple, cored

¼ tsp vanilla extract

Preparation:

Place the blueberries in a colander. Rinse well under cold running water and drain. Set aside.

Peel the grapefruit and divide into wedges. Cut each wedge in half and set aside.

Peel the avocado and cut lengthwise in half. Remove the pit and cut into small cubes. Fill the measuring cup and reserve the rest in the refrigerator.

Wash the apple and cut lengthwise in half. Remove the core and cut into bite-sized pieces. Set aside.

Now, combine blueberries, grapefruit, avocado, and apple in a juicer and process until juiced. Transfer to a serving glass and stir in the vanilla extract. Refrigerate for 10 minutes before serving.

Nutrition information per serving: Kcal: 436, Protein: 6.4g, Carbs: 69.5g, Fats: 23.2g

5. Orange Carrot Juice

Ingredients:

1 large orange, peeled

1 large carrot, sliced

1 cup butternut squash, cubed

1 whole lemon, peeled

1 cup cucumber, sliced

¼ tsp turmeric, ground

Preparation:

Peel the orange and divide into wedges. Cut each wedge in half and set aside.

Wash and peel the carrot. Cut into thin slices and set aside.

Wash the squash and chop into small cubes. Fill the measuring cup and reserve the rest in the refrigerator. Set aside.

Peel the lemon and cut lengthwise in half. Set aside.

Wash the cucumber and cut into thin slices. Fill the measuring cup and reserve the rest for later.

Now, combine orange, carrot, squash, lemon, and

cucumber in a juicer and process until juiced. Transfer to a serving glass and stir in the turmeric.

Add some crushed ice and serve immediately.

Nutrition information per serving: Kcal: 127, Protein: 4.6g, Carbs: 40.7g, Fats: 0.9g

6. Lemon Banana Juice

Ingredients:

1 cup strawberries, chopped

1 whole lemon, peeled

1 large banana, chunked

1 cup pineapple, chunked

1 tbsp fresh mint, finely chopped

Preparation:

Peel the lemon and cut lengthwise in half. Set aside.

Peel the banana and cut into small chunks. Set aside.

Wash the strawberries and remove the stems. Chop into small pieces and fill the measuring cup. Reserve the rest in the refrigerator.

Cut the top of the pineapple using a sharp paring knife. Gently remove all hard skin and slice it into thin slices. Fill the measuring cup and reserve the rest for later.

Now, combine lemon, banana, strawberries, and pineapple in a juicer. Process until juiced. Transfer to a serving glass and stir in the mint.

Add few ice cubes and serve immediately.

Nutrition information per serving: Kcal: 224, Protein: 4.1g, Carbs: 69.4g, Fats: 1.3g

7. Celery Cherry Juice

Ingredients:

1 cup celery, chopped

1 cup cherries, pitted

1 cup watermelon, diced

1 small ginger knob, peeled

1 oz water

¼ tsp cinnamon, ground

Preparation:

Wash the celery and cut into small pieces. Fill the measuring cup and reserve the rest for later. Set aside.

Rinse the cherries under cold running water using a colander. Drain and cut each in half. Remove the pits and set aside.

Cut the watermelon in half. Cut one large wedge and wrap the rest in a plastic foil and refrigerate. Dice the wedge and remove the pits. Fill the measuring cup and set aside.

Peel the ginger knob and cut into small pieces. Set aside.

Now, combine celery, cherries, watermelon, and ginger

knob in a juicer and process until juiced. Transfer to a serving glass and stir in the water and cinnamon. Add some ice and serve immediately.

Nutrition information per serving: Kcal: 143, Protein: 3.4g, Carbs: 40.2g, Fats: 0.7g

8. Pear Lemon Juice

Ingredients:

1 small pear, chopped

1 whole lemon, peeled and halved

1 cup of apricots, pitted and halved

1 tbsp liquid honey

1 small Granny Smith's apple, cored

1 cup fresh mint, torn

Preparation:

Wash the pear and cut in half. Remove the core and cut into small pieces. Set aside.

Peel the lemon and cut lengthwise in half. Set aside.

Wash the apricots and cut each lengthwise in half. Remove the pits and fill the measuring cup. Reserve the rest in the refrigerator for some other juice.

Wash the apple and cut lengthwise in half. Remove the core and chop into bite-sized pieces. Set aside.

Rinse the mint thoroughly under cold running water. Drain and torn into small pieces. Set aside.

Now, combine pear, lemon, apricots, apple, and mint in a

juicer and process until well juiced. Transfer to a serving glass and add some ice before serving.

Enjoy!

Nutrition information per serving: Kcal: 217, Protein: 4.9g, Carbs: 68.5g, Fats: 1.5g

9. Melon Apple Juice

Ingredients:

1 large honeydew melon wedge, chopped

1 medium-sized Zestar apple, cored

2 cups blueberries

2 oz coconut water

1 tbsp mint, finely chopped

Preparation:

Cut melon lengthwise in half. Scoop out the seeds and then wash. Cut one large wedge and peel it. Cut into small cubes and set aside.

Wash the apple and cut lengthwise in half. Remove the core and cut into bite-sized pieces. Set aside.

Place the blueberries in a large colander. Rinse well under cold running water and drain. Set aside.

Now, combine honeydew melon, apple, and blueberries in a juicer. Process until juiced.

Transfer to a serving glass and stir in the coconut water, vanilla extract, and mint. Add some crushed ice and serve immediately.

Nutrition information per serving: Kcal: 283, Protein: 3.7g, Carbs: 85.1g, Fats: 1.5g

10. Kiwi Apple Juice

Ingredients:

1 cup celery, chopped

1 whole kiwi, peeled

1 medium-sized Golden Delicious apple, cored

1 medium-sized orange, peeled

1 tbsp liquid honey

¼ tsp ginger, ground

Preparation:

Peel the kiwi and cut lengthwise in half. Set aside.

Wash the apple and cut lengthwise in half. Remove the core and cut into bite-sized pieces. Set aside.

Wash the celery and chop into small pieces. Fill the measuring cup and reserve the rest for later. Set aside.

Peel the orange and divide into wedges. Cut each wedge in half and set aside.

Now, combine kiwi, apple, celery, and orange in a juicer and process until juiced. Transfer to a serving glass and stir in the honey and ginger.

Refrigerate for 15 minutes before serving.

Enjoy!

Nutrition information per serving: Kcal: 172, Protein: 3.5g, Carbs: 51.2g, Fats: 1.1g

11. Apple Nutmeg Juice

Ingredients:

1 large green apple, cored

¼ tsp nutmeg, ground

1 cup cranberries

1 large pear, cored

3 large strawberries, chopped

1 large orange, peeled

2 oz coconut water

Preparation:

Wash the apple and cut in half. Remove the core and cut into bite-sized pieces. Set aside.

Wash the cranberries thoroughly under cold running water. Drain and set aside.

Wash the pear and cut lengthwise in half. Remove the core and cut into bite-sized pieces. Set aside.

Wash the strawberries thoroughly and chop into small pieces. Set aside.

Peel the orange and divide into wedges. Set aside.

Now, combine apple, cranberries, pear, strawberries, orange, and nutmeg in a juicer. Process until well juiced and transfer to serving glasses.

Stir in the water and refrigerate or add some ice before serving.

Nutritional information per serving: Kcal: 158, Protein: 4.7g, Carbs: 47.9g, Fats: 1.1g

12. Peach Gala Juice

Ingredients:

2 large peaches, pitted

1 large Gala apple, cored

1 cup watermelon, cubed

5 fresh cherries, pitted

3 oz coconut water

Preparation:

Wash the peaches and cut in half. Remove the pits and cut into bite-sized pieces. Set aside.

Wash the apple and cut in half. Remove the core and cut into bite-sized pieces. Set aside.

Cut the watermelon lengthwise. For one cup, you will need about one large wedge. Peel and cut into chunks. Remove the seeds and set aside. Reserve the rest of the melon for some other juices.

Wash the cherries and cut in half. Remove the pits and set aside.

Now, process peaches, apple, watermelon, and cherries in a juicer. Transfer to serving glasses and stir in the coconut water. Add some ice and serve immediately.

Nutritional information per serving: Kcal: 276, Protein: 5.4g, Carbs: 47.6g, Fats: 1.6g

13. Leek Lime Juice

Ingredients:

3 large leeks, chopped

1 large lime, peeled

1 cup cauliflower, chopped

1 large zucchini, chopped

2 oz water

Preparation:

Wash the leeks and cut into small pieces. Set aside.

Peel the lime and cut lengthwise in half. Set aside.

Trim off the outer leaves of cauliflower. Wash it and cut into small pieces. Set aside.

Peel the zucchini and cut in half. Scrape out the seeds and cut into small chunks. Set aside.

Now, combine leeks, lime, cauliflower, and zucchini in a juicer. Process until well juiced and stir in the water. Refrigerate for 10 minutes before serving.

Enjoy!

Nutritional information per serving: Kcal: 241, Protein: 13.2g, Carbs: 64.7g, Fats: 2.6g

14. Apricot Pomegranate Juice

Ingredients:

1 cup of pomegranate seeds

1 large lemon, peeled

1 large apricot, pitted

1 large orange, wedged

1 large carrot, sliced

2 oz coconut water

Preparation:

Cut the top of the pomegranate fruit using a sharp knife. Slice down to each of the white membranes inside of the fruit. Pop the seeds into measuring cup and set aside.

Peel the lemon and cut lengthwise in half. Set aside.

Wash the apricot and cut in half. Remove the pit and cut into small pieces. Set aside.

Peel the orange and divide into wedges. Set aside.

Peel and wash the carrot. Cut into thin slices and set aside.

Now, combine pomegranate seeds, lemon, apricot, orange, and carrot in a juicer. Process until well juiced and transfer to serving glasses. Stir in the coconut water and add few ice cubes before serving.

Nutritional information per serving: Kcal: 241, Protein: 7.3g, Carbs: 73.9g, Fats: 2.3g

15. Kale Parsley Juice

Ingredients:

1 cup fresh kale, torn

1 cup fresh parsley, torn

2 cups broccoli, trimmed

1 large green apple, chopped

1 cup fresh spinach, torn

2 oz water

Preparation:

Wash the broccoli under cold running water and cut into small pieces. Set aside.

Combine kale, parsley, and spinach in a colander and rinse under cold running water. Drain and torn with hands. Set aside.

Wash the apple and cut in half. Remove the core and cut into bite-sized pieces. Set aside.

Now, combine kale, parsley, broccoli, apple, and spinach in a juicer. Process until well juiced and stir in the water.

Refrigerate for 10 minutes before serving.

Nutritional information per serving: Kcal: 223, Protein: 20.4g, Carbs: 62.1g, Fats: 3.5g

16. Apple Strawberry Juice

Ingredients:

1 large red apple, cored

2 large strawberries, chopped

2 large grapefruits, peeled

1 small ginger knob, peeled

2 oz coconut water

Preparation:

Wash the apple and cut in half. Remove the core and cut into bite-sized pieces. Set aside.

Wash the strawberries and cut into small pieces. Set aside.

Peel the grapefruits and divide into wedges. Set aside.

Peel the ginger knob and set aside.

Now, combine apple, strawberries, grapefruits, and ginger in a juicer. Process until well juiced and transfer to serving glasses. Stir in the coconut water and refrigerate for 20 minutes, or add some ice before serving.

Nutritional information per serving: Kcal: 302, Protein: 4.8g, Carbs: 86.3g, Fats: 1.7g

17. Peach Apple Juice

Ingredients:

2 large peaches, pitted

1 large Red Delicious apple, cored

1 cup strawberries, chopped

1 large lemon, peeled

1 large kiwi, peeled

1 large orange, peeled

2 oz water

Preparation:

Wash the peaches and cut in half. Remove the pits and cut into small pieces. Set aside.

Wash the apple and cut half. Remove the core and cut into bite-sized pieces. Set aside.

Wash the strawberries under cold running water. Remove the green parts and cut into bite-sized pieces. Set aside.

Peel the lemon and kiwi. Cut lengthwise in half and set aside.

Now, combine peaches, apple, strawberries, lemon, and kiwi in a juicer and process until well juiced. Transfer to serving glasses and stir in the water. Add some ice and serve immediately.

Enjoy!

Nutritional information per serving: Kcal: 345, Protein: 7.8g, Carbs: 105g, Fats: 2.3g

18. Raspberry Apricot Juice

Ingredients:

1 cup raspberries

3 large apricots, pitted

1 cup blackberries

1 large Gala apple, cored

3 large carrots, peeled

Preparation:

Combine raspberries and blackberries in a large colander. Rinse under cold running water and slightly drain. Set aside.

Wash the apricots and cut in half. Remove the pits and cut into bite-sized pieces. Set aside.

Wash the apple and cut in half. Remove the core and cut into small pieces.

Wash and peel the carrots. Cut into thin slices and set aside.

Now, combine raspberries, apricots, blackberries, apple, and carrots in a juicer. Process until well juiced and transfer to serving glasses. Stir in the water and refrigerate for 10-15 minutes before serving.

Enjoy!

Nutritional information per serving: Kcal: 301, Protein: 7.6g, Carbs: 97.4g, Fats: 2.9g

19. Kiwi Lime Juice

Ingredients:

3 large kiwis, peeled

1 large lime, peeled

1 large zucchini, seeded

1 cup pomegranate seeds

1 large orange, peeled

Preparation:

Peel the kiwis and lime. Cut lengthwise in half and set aside.

Wash the zucchini and cut in half. Scoop out the seeds using a spoon. Cut into small chunks and set aside.

Cut the top of the pomegranate fruit using a sharp knife. Slice down to each of the white membranes inside of the fruit. Pop the seeds into a measuring cup and set aside.

Peel the orange and divide into wedges. Set aside.

Now, process kiwis, lime, zucchini, pomegranate seeds, and orange in a juicer.

Transfer to a serving glasses and add some ice cubes before serving.

Nutritional information per serving: Kcal: 183, Protein: 8.5g, Carbs: 52.6g, Fats: 1.6g

20. Blueberry Cucumber Juice

Ingredients:

1 cup blueberries

1 large cucumber, sliced

1 cup mango, chopped

1 large Zestar apple, cored

2 oz water

¼ tsp vanilla extract

Preparation:

Place the blueberries in a colander and wash under cold running water. Drain and set aside.

Wash the cucumber and cut into thin slices. Set aside.

Wash the mango and cut into chunks. Fill the measuring cup and reserve the rest for some other juice. Set aside.

Wash the apple and remove the core. Cut into bite-sized pieces and set aside.

Now, combine blueberries, cucumber, mango, and apple in a juicer and process until juiced.

Transfer to serving glasses and stir in the water and vanilla extract. Add some ice before serving and enjoy!

Nutritional information per serving: Kcal: 180, Protein: 5.9g, Carbs: 63.5g, Fats: 1.1g

21. Carrot Watercress Juice

Ingredients:

2 large carrots, sliced

1 cup watercress, torn

1 cup pineapple, chunked

1 large lime, peeled

1 small ginger knob, peeled

2 oz water

Preparation:

Wash and peel the carrots. Cut into thin slices and set aside.

Wash the watercress thoroughly under cold running water. Torn with hands and set aside.

Peel the pineapple and cut into small chunks. Set aside.

Peel the lime and cut lengthwise in half. Set aside.

Peel the ginger root knob and cut into small pieces. Set aside.

Now, combine carrots, watercress, pineapple, lemon, and ginger in a juicer and process until well juiced.

Transfer to serving glasses and stir in water.

Add some ice and serve.

Nutritional information per serving: Kcal: 135, Protein: 3.3g, Carbs: 40.6g, Fats: 3.3g

22. Lime Celery Juice

Ingredients:

1 large lime, peeled

2 large celery stalks, chopped

2 large grapefruits, peeled

1 large kiwi, peeled

1 cup red leaf lettuce, chopped

2 oz water

Preparation:

Peel the lime and kiwi. Cut in half and set aside.

Wash and chop the celery stalks into small pieces. Set aside.

Peel the grapefruit and divide into wedges. Set aside.

Rinse the lettuce thoroughly under cold running water and roughly chop it. Set aside.

Now, combine lime, celery, grapefruit, kiwi, and lettuce in a juicer and process until well juiced.

Transfer to serving glasses and stir in the water. Serve immediately.

Nutritional information per serving: Kcal: 233, Protein: 6g, Carbs: 70.7g, Fats: 1.3g

23. Apricot Pomegranate Juice

Ingredients:

2 large apricots, pitted

1 cup pomegranate seeds

2 large oranges, peeled

1 cup green grapes

1 large lemon, peeled

1 small ginger slice, peeled

Preparation:

Wash the apricots and cut in half. Remove the pits and cut into small pieces. Set aside.

Cut the top of the pomegranate fruit using a sharp knife. Slice down to each of the white membranes inside of the fruit. Pop the seeds into a measuring cup and set aside.

Peel the oranges and divide into wedges. Set aside.

Peel the lemon and cut lengthwise in half. Set aside.

Peel the ginger slice and set aside.

Now, combine apricots, pomegranate, oranges, lemon, and ginger in a juicer. Process until well juiced and transfer to serving glasses. Refrigerate for 10 minutes before serving.

Nutritional information per serving: Kcal: 294, Protein: 7.2g, Carbs: 88.9g, Fats: 2.3g

24. Orange Raspberry Juice

Ingredients:

1 large orange, peeled

1 cup raspberries

2 cups watermelon, chopped

1 large kiwi, peeled

2 oz coconut water

Preparation:

Peel the orange and divide into wedges. Set aside.

Wash the raspberries thoroughly under cold running water. Drain and set aside.

Cut the watermelon lengthwise. For 2 cups, you will need about two large wedges. Peel and cut into chunks. Remove the seeds and set aside. Reserve the rest of the melon for some other juices. Set aside.

Peel the kiwi and cut lengthwise in half. Set aside.

Now, combine watermelon, orange, raspberries, and kiwi in a juicer. Process until juiced and transfer to serving glasses. Stir in the coconut water and refrigerate for 10 minutes before serving.

Nutritional information per serving: Kcal: 232, Protein: 5.8g, Carbs: 71.4g, Fats: 1.8g

25. Sour Apple Mint Juice

Ingredients:

1 large green apple, cored

1 tbsp fresh mint, chopped

1 large papaya, peeled and chopped

1 cup pomegranate seeds

2 oz water

Preparation:

Wash the apple and cut in half. Using a sharp knife, remove the core and cut into bite-sized pieces. Set aside.

Peel the papaya and cut lengthwise in half. Scoop out the black seeds and flesh using a spoon. Cut into small chunks and set aside.

Cut the top of the pomegranate fruit using a sharp knife. Slice down to each of the white membranes inside of the fruit. Pop the seeds into a measuring cup and set aside.

Now, combine apple, mint, papaya, and pomegranate in a juicer. Process until well juiced and transfer to serving glasses. Stir in the water and refrigerate before serving.

Nutritional information per serving: Kcal: 438, Protein: 6.1g, Carbs: 129g, Fats: 3.4g

26. Lime Guava Juice

Ingredients:

1 cup pineapple, chopped

2 large limes, peeled

1 cup guava, chopped

1 large cucumber, sliced

1 tbsp fresh mint, chopped

2 oz water

Preparation:

Peel the limes and cut lengthwise in half. Set aside.

Wash the guava and cut into chunks. Fill the measuring cup and reserve the rest for some other recipe in a refrigerator.

Cut the top of a pineapple and peel it using a sharp knife. Cut into small chunks and fill the measuring cup. Reserve the rest of the pineapple in a refrigerator.

Wash the cucumber and cut into thin slices. Set aside.

Now, combine limes, guava, pineapple, cucumber, and mint in a juicer. Process until well juiced and transfer to serving glasses. Stir in the water and refrigerate for 15 minutes before serving.

Nutritional information per serving: Kcal: 158, Protein: 4.7g, Carbs: 47.9g, Fats: 1.1g

27. Apple Asparagus Juice

Ingredients:

1 large red apple, cored

1 cup asparagus, trimmed

1 cup fresh spinach, torn

1 cup collard greens, torn

1 cup mustard greens, torn

2 oz water

Preparation:

Wash the apple and cut in half. Remove the core and cut into bite-sized pieces. Set aside.

Trim off the woody ends of the asparagus. Rinse well and cut into bite-sized pieces. Set aside.

Combine spinach, collard greens, and mustard greens in a large colander. Wash under cold running water and drain. Torn with hands and set aside.

Now, combine apple, asparagus, spinach, collard greens, and mustard greens in a juicer and process until well juiced. Transfer to serving glasses and stir in the water. Refrigerate for 15 minutes before serving.

Enjoy!

Nutritional information per serving: Kcal: 207, Protein: 16.1g, Carbs: 58.6g, Fats: 2.5g

28. Apple Beet Juice

Ingredients:

1 large Red Delicious apple, cored

1 cup beets, chopped

2 cups raspberries

1 cup fresh mint, torn

1 large lemon, peeled

3 oz water

Preparation:

Wash the apple and cut in half. Remove the core and cut into bite-sized pieces. Set aside.

Wash the beets and trim off the green ends. Cut into small pieces and fill the measuring cup. Reserve the greens for some other juice.

Wash the raspberries under cold running water using a colander. Drain and set aside.

Rinse the mint thoroughly under cold running water and torn with hands. Set aside.

Peel the lemon and cut lengthwise in half. Set aside.

Now, combine apple, beets, raspberries, mint, and lemon

in a juicer. Process until well juiced. Stir in the water and refrigerate for 10 minutes before serving.

Enjoy!

Nutritional information per serving: Kcal: 218, Protein: 7.5g, Carbs: 76.4g, Fats: 2.5g

29. Guava Lime Juice

Ingredients:

1 large lime, peeled

2 large oranges, peeled

1 large guava, peeled

1 large cucumber, sliced

2 oz water

1 tsp agave nectar

Preparation:

Peel the lime and cut lengthwise in half. Set aside.

Peel the oranges and divide into wedges. Set aside.

Peel and wash the guava. Cut into small chunks and set aside.

Wash the cucumber and cut into thin slices. Set aside.

Now, combine lime, orange, guava, and cucumber in a juicer and process until juiced.

Transfer to serving glasses and stir in the water and agave nectar. Add some ice and serve immediately.

Nutritional information per serving: Kcal: 210, Protein: 7g, Carbs: 65.7g, Fats: 1.3g

30. Spinach Lemon Juice

Ingredients:

1 cup fresh spinach, chopped

1 large lemon, peeled

1 cup celery, chopped

1 cup fresh mint, chopped

2 oz water

Preparation:

Wash the spinach and mint in a colander. Chop and place in a medium bowl. Set aside.

Peel the lemon and cut lengthwise in half. Set aside.

Wash the celery stalks and chop into small pieces. Fill the measuring cup and set aside.

Now, combine spinach, lemon, celery, and mint in a juicer and process until juiced. Transfer to serving glasses and stir in the water.

Refrigerate for 5 minutes before serving.

Nutritional information per serving: Kcal: 35, Protein: 3.1g, Carbs: 13.2g, Fats: 0.7g

31. Pear Pepper Juice

Ingredients:

1 large pear, cored

1 large red bell pepper, chopped

2 cups beets, chopped

1 large lemon, peeled

1 small ginger root slice, peeled

3 oz water

Preparation:

Wash the pear and cut in half. Remove the core and cut into bite-sized pieces. Set aside.

Wash the bell pepper and cut in half. Remove the seeds and cut into small pieces. Set aside.

Wash the beets and trim off the green ends. Cut into small pieces and fill the measuring cup. Reserve the greens for some other juice. Set aside.

Peel the lemon and cut lengthwise in half. Set aside.

Peel the ginger slice and cut in half. Set aside.

Now, combine pear, bell pepper, beets, lemon, and ginger in a juicer. Process until well juiced and transfer to serving glasses.

Stir in the water and add some ice before serving.

Enjoy!

Nutritional information per serving: Kcal: 239, Protein: 7.5g, Carbs: 76.7g, Fats: 1.4g

32. Apple Cinnamon Juice

Ingredients:

1 large Granny Smith's apple, cored

¼ tsp cinnamon, ground

2 cups pumpkin, cubed

1 large cucumber, sliced

1 cup Swiss chard, torn

2 oz water

Preparation:

Wash the apple and cut in half. Remove the core and cut into bite-sized pieces. Set aside.

Peel the pumpkin and cut in half. Scoop out the seeds using a spoon. Cut one large wedge and peel it. Cut into small cubes and fill the measuring cup. Reserve the rest for some other juice.

Wash the cucumber and cut into thin slices. Set aside.

Wash the Swiss chard thoroughly under cold running water. Drain and torn with hands. Set aside.

Now, combine apple, pumpkin, cucumber, and Swiss chards in a juicer. Process until well juiced and stir in the water and nutmeg.

Refrigerate for 10 minutes before serving.

Nutritional information per serving: Kcal: 196, Protein: 5.8g, Carbs: 55.4g, Fats: 1.1g

33. Pomegranate Plum Juice

Ingredients:

1 cup pomegranate seeds

4 large plums, pitted

1 large red bell pepper, chopped

1 cup cranberries

1 large Gala apple, cored

Preparation:

Cut the top of the pomegranate fruit using a sharp knife. Slice down to each of the white membranes inside of the fruit. Pop the seeds into a measuring cup and set aside.

Wash the plums and cut in half. Remove the pits and cut into bite-sized pieces. Set aside.

Wash the bell pepper and cut lengthwise in half. Remove the seeds and cut into small pieces. Set aside.

Wash the cranberries thoroughly and drain. Set aside.

Wash the apple and cut in half. Remove the core and cut into bite-sized pieces. Set aside.

Now, combine pomegranate, plums, cranberries, and apple in a juicer. Process until well juiced and add some ice before serving.

Enjoy!

Nutritional information per serving: Kcal: 277, Protein: 6g, Carbs: 83g, Fats: 1.4g

34. Blackberry Cucumber Juice

Ingredients:

1 cup blackberries

1 large cucumber, sliced

5 large plums, pitted

1 cup green cabbage, chopped

2 oz water

Preparation:

Rinse the blackberries under cold running water using a colander. Slightly drain and set aside.

Wash the cucumber and cut into thin slices. Set aside.

Wash the plums and cut in half. Remove the pits and cut into quarters. Set aside.

Wash the cabbage thoroughly under cold running water. Drain and roughly chop it. Set aside.

Now, combine blackberries, cucumber, plums, and cabbage in a juicer and process until juice. Transfer to serving glasses and stir in the water. Refrigerate for 10 minutes before serving.

Nutritional information per serving: Kcal: 221, Protein: 7.5g, Carbs: 69.1g, Fats: 2.1g

35. Lemon Lime Juice

Ingredients:

1 large lemon, peeled

1 large lime, peeled

1 large artichoke, chopped

1 medium-sized zucchini, chopped

1 cup fresh mint, chopped

1 cup purple cabbage, chopped

2 oz water

Preparation:

Peel the lemon and lime. Cut lengthwise in half and set aside.

Trim off the outer leaves of the artichoke. Wash it and cut into bite-sized pieces. Set aside.

Peel the zucchini and cut lengthwise in half. Scoop out the seeds and peel it. Cut into bite-sized pieces and set aside.

Combine mint and cabbage in a colander. Rinse thoroughly under cold running water and roughly chop it. Set aside.

Now, combine lemon, lime, artichoke, zucchini, basil, and

cabbage in a juicer. Process until well juiced and stir in the water.

Refrigerate for 15 minutes before serving.

Enjoy!

Nutritional information per serving: Kcal: 104, Protein: 10.4g, Carbs: 38.1g, Fats: 1.3g

36. Green Salty Juice

Ingredients:

1 cup watercress, torn

1 cup collard greens, torn

1 cup asparagus, trimmed

1 green bell pepper, chopped

1 large cucumber, sliced

2 oz water

¼ tsp salt

Preparation:

Combine watercress and collard greens in a colander. Wash thoroughly under cold running water and torn with hands. Set aside.

Wash the asparagus and trim off the woody ends. Cut into bite-sized pieces and fill the measuring cup. Reserve the rest for some other juice.

Wash the bell pepper and lengthwise in half. Remove the seeds and chop into small pieces. Set aside.

Wash the cucumber and cut into thin slices. Set aside.

Now, combine watercress, collard greens, asparagus, bell

pepper, and cucumber in a juicer and process until well juiced. Transfer to serving glasses and stir in the salt and water. Refrigerate for 10-15 minutes before serving.

Nutritional information per serving: Kcal: 86, Protein: 8.2g, Carbs: 26.1g, Fats: 1g

37. Asparagus Lemon Juice

Ingredients:

1 cup fresh asparagus, trimmed and chopped

1 whole lemon, peeled

1 cup pomegranate seeds

1 tbsp liquid honey

1 oz water

Preparation:

Wash the asparagus and trim off the woody ends. Cut into bite-sized pieces and set aside.

Peel the lemon and cut into quarters. Set aside.

Cut the top of the pomegranate fruit using a sharp paring knife. Slice down to each of the white membranes inside of the fruit. Pop the seeds into a measuring cup and set aside.

Now, combine asparagus, lemon, and pomegranate seeds in a juicer and process until well juiced. Transfer to a serving glass and stir in the honey and water.

Add some ice and enjoy!

Nutritional information per serving: Kcal: 145, Protein: 5.1g, Carbs: 26.8g, Fats: 1.3g

38. Blueberry Lime Juice

Ingredients:

2 cups blueberries

1 whole lime, peeled

1 cup watermelon, cubed

1 cup fresh mint, torn

¼ tsp cayenne pepper, ground

1 oz water

Preparation:

Place the blueberries in a large colander. Rinse well under cold running water and set aside.

Peel the lime and cut lengthwise in half. Set aside.

Cut one large watermelon wedge. Using a sharp paring knife, peel and cut into small cubes. Remove the seeds and set aside.

Rinse the basil and roughly torn it with hands. Set aside.

Now, combine blueberries, lime, watermelon, and basil in a juicer. Process until juiced. Transfer to a serving glass and stir in the cayenne pepper and water.

Refrigerate for 5 minutes before serving.

Nutritional information per serving: Kcal: 198, Protein: 4.1g, Carbs: 58.7g, Fats: 1.4g

39. Mango Mint Juice

Ingredients:

1 cup mango, cut into chunks

1 cup fresh mint, roughly chopped

1 whole grapefruit, peeled

1 large banana, peeled

2 large strawberries, chopped

Preparation:

Peel the mango and cut into small chunks. Fill the measuring cup and reserve the rest in the refrigerator. Set aside.

Rinse the mint roughly and torn with hands. Set aside.

Peel the grapefruit and divide into wedges. Cut each wedge in half and set aside.

Peel the banana and cut into small pieces. Set aside.

Wash the strawberries and remove the stems. Cut into bite-sized pieces and set aside.

Now, combine mango, mint, grapefruit, banana, and strawberries in a juicer and process until juiced. Transfer to a serving glass and add some ice cubes before serving.

Enjoy!

Nutritional information per serving: Kcal: 301, Protein: 5.9g, Carbs: 88.5g, Fats: 1.7g

40. Beet Orange Juice

Ingredients:

1 whole beet, sliced

1 small mandarin orange, wedged

1 cup pineapple, chunked

2 tbsp coconut water

¼ tsp ginger, ground

Preparation:

Wash and trim off the beet. Cut into small slices and set aside.

Peel the orange and divide into wedges. Cut each wedge in half and set aside.

Cut the top of a pineapple and peel it using a sharp paring knife. Cut into small chunks and fill the measuring cup. Reserve the rest of the pineapple in a refrigerator.

Now, combine beet, orange, and pineapple in a juicer and process until juiced. Transfer to a serving glass and stir in the coconut water and ginger.

Add some crushed ice and serve immediately.

Nutritional information per serving: Kcal: 135, Protein: 3.1g, Carbs: 40.7g, Fats: 0.5g

41. Kale Mint Juice

Ingredients:

1 cup celery, chopped

1 cup fresh kale, torn

1 cup fresh mint, torn

1 whole lime, peeled

1 small Granny Smith's apple, cored

Preparation:

Combine kale and mint in a large colander. Wash thoroughly under cold running water. Slightly drain and torn with hands. Set aside.

Wash the celery and chop into small pieces. Fill the measuring cup and set aside.

Peel the lime and cut into small pieces. Set aside.

Wash the apple and cut in half. Remove the core and cut into bite-sized pieces. Set aside.

Now, combine kale, mint, celery, lime, and apple in a juicer and process until juiced. Transfer to a serving glass and add some ice before serving.

Enjoy!

Nutritional information per serving: Kcal: 121, Protein: 5.3g, Carbs: 35.8g, Fats: 1.3g

42. Celery Zestar Juice

Ingredients:

2 medium-sized celery stalk, chopped

1 small Zestar apple, cored

1 cup fresh kale, chopped

1 cup Romaine lettuce, shredded

Preparation:

Wash the celery stalks and cut into bite-sized pieces. Set aside.

Wash the apple and cut in half. Remove the core and cut into small pieces. Set aside.

Wash the kale thoroughly under cold running water. Slightly drain and chop it into small pieces. Set aside.

Wash the lettuce leaves and shred it. Fill the measuring cup and reserve the rest for later.

Now, combine celery, apple, kale, and lettuce in a juicer and process until juiced. Transfer to a serving glass and add some ice before serving.

Enjoy!

Nutritional information per serving: Kcal: 103, Protein: 4.6g, Carbs: 29.4g, Fats: 1.2g

43. Green Ginger Juice

Ingredients:

1 cup collard greens, chopped

2 cups Swiss chard, chopped

1 cup fresh kale, chopped

1 whole lemon, peeled

1 cup cucumber, sliced

¼ tsp ginger, ground

Preparation:

Combine collard greens, Swiss chard, and kale in a large colander. Rinse thoroughly under cold running water. Slightly drain and roughly chop all. Set aside.

Peel the lemon and cut lengthwise in half. Set aside.

Wash the cucumber and cut into thin slices. Fill the measuring cup and reserve the rest in the refrigerator. Set aside.

Now, combine Swiss chard, kale, collard greens, lemon, and cucumber in a juicer. Process until juiced.

Transfer to a serving glass and stir in the ginger.

Serve cold.

Nutritional information per serving: Kcal: 57, Protein: 6.3g, Carbs: 17.8g, Fats: 1.2g

44. Broccoli Cucumber Juice

Ingredients:

1 cup of broccoli, chopped

1 cup of cucumber, sliced

1 large red bell pepper, chopped

1 large celery stalk, chopped

¼ tsp of ginger, ground

Preparation:

Wash the broccoli and trim off the outer wilted layers. Cut into small pieces and set aside.

Wash the cucumber and cut into thin slices. Fill the measuring cup and reserve the rest in the refrigerator.

Wash the pepper and cut in half. Remove the seeds and stem. Cut into thin slices and set aside.

Wash the celery stalk and cut into small pieces. Set aside.

Now, combine pepper, broccoli, cucumber, and celery in a juicer and process until well juiced. Transfer to a serving glass and stir in the ginger.

Refrigerate for 10 minutes before serving.

Nutritional information per serving: Kcal: 71, Protein: 4.9g, Carbs: 19.7g, Fats: 1g

45. Brussels Sprout Carrot Juice

Ingredients:

1 cup of Brussels sprouts, trimmed

1 large carrot, sliced

1 large artichoke, peeled and chopped

1 cup of fresh celery, chopped

1 cup of turnip greens, chopped

1 large green apple, cored

½ tsp of turmeric, ground

2 oz of water

Preparation:

Trim off the outer leaves of the Brussels sprouts and wash them thoroughly. Cut in half and set aside.

Wash the carrot and cut into thin slices. Set aside. Using a sharp knife, trim off the outer leaves of the artichoke. Cut into small pieces and set aside.

Wash the celery and chop it into bite-sized pieces. Set aside.

Wash the apple and cut in half. Remove the core and cut into bite-sized pieces. Set aside.

Wash the turnip greens thoroughly and torn with hands. Set aside.

Now, combine Brussels sprouts, carrot, artichoke, celery, turnip greens, and apple in a juicer. Process until well juiced and transfer to serving glasses. Stir in the turmeric and water. Add some ice before serving.

Nutritional information per serving: Kcal: 205, Protein: 11.3g, Carbs: 66.7g, Fats: 1.4g

46. Butternut Squash Parsnip Juice

Ingredients:

3 large red bell peppers, chopped

1 cup of butternut squash, cubed

1 cup of parsnip, sliced

1 tbsp of fresh parsley, chopped

¼ tsp salt

2 oz of water

Preparation:

Peel the butternut squash and remove the seeds using a spoon. Cut into small cubes and fill the measuring cup. Reserve the rest of the squash for some other recipe. Wrap in a plastic foil and refrigerate.

Wash the parsnip and peel it. Cut into thin slices and set aside.

Wash the red bell peppers and cut lengthwise in half. Remove the seeds and chop into small pieces.

Now, combine butternut squash, parsnip, bell peppers, and parsley in a juicer. Process until well juiced and transfer to serving glasses. Stir in the water and salt. Add some ice and serve immediately.

Nutritional information per serving: Kcal: 238, Protein: 7.9g, Carbs: 70.2g, Fats: 2.1g

47. Apple Mango Juice

Ingredients:

1 medium-sized apple, cored

1 cup mango, chunked

1 cup of pomegranate seeds

1 small ginger slice

¼ tsp cinnamon, ground

1 oz water

Preparation:

Wash the apple and cut lengthwise in half. Remove the core and cut into small pieces. Set aside.

Peel the mango and cut into chunks. Fill the measuring cup and reserve the rest in the refrigerator. Set aside.

Cut the top of the pomegranate fruit using a sharp paring knife. Slice down to each of the white membranes inside of the fruit. Pop the seeds into a measuring cup and set aside.

Peel the ginger slice and chop into small pieces. Set aside.

Now, combine apple, mango, pomegranate seeds, and ginger in a juicer and process until juiced. Transfer to a serving glass and stir in the cinnamon and water.

Refrigerate for 10 minutes before serving.

Nutrition information per serving: Kcal: 227, Protein: 3.6g, Carbs: 64.1g, Fats: 1.9g

48.   Carrot Watercress Juice

Ingredients:

1 large carrot, sliced

1 cup watercress, torn

1 cup pumpkin, cubed

1 small Golden Delicious apple, cored and chopped

1 whole lemon, peeled

Preparation:

Wash and peel the carrot. Cut into thin slices and set aside.

Rinse the watercress thoroughly under cold running water. Drain and torn into small pieces. Set aside.

Cut the top of a pumpkin. Cut lengthwise in half and then scrape out the seeds. Cut one large wedge and peel it. Cut into small cubes and fill the measuring cup. Reserve the rest in the refrigerator.

Wash the apple and cut lengthwise in half. Remove the core and cut into bite-sized pieces. Set aside.

Peel the lemon and cut lengthwise in half. Set aside.

Now, combine carrot, watercress, pumpkin, apple, and

lemon in a juicer and process until juiced. Transfer to a serving glass and add some ice before serving.

Enjoy!

Nutrition information per serving: Kcal: 126, Protein: 3.6g, Carbs: 37.8g, Fats: 0.7g

49. Pineapple Spinach Juice

Ingredients:

1 cup pineapple, chunked

1 cup spinach, chopped

1 cup cherries, pitted

1 whole lemon, peeled

¼ tsp cinnamon, ground

1 oz water

Preparation:

Using a sharp paring knife, cut the top of the pineapple. Gently remove all hard skin and slice it into thin slices. Fill the measuring cup and reserve the rest for later.

Rinse the spinach thoroughly under cold running water. Drain and chop into small pieces. Set aside.

Place the cherries in a medium colander. Rinse well under cold running water and remove the stems, if any. Cut each in half and remove the pits. Fill the measuring cup and reserve the rest in the refrigerator.

Peel the lemon and cut lengthwise in half. Set aside.

Now, combine pineapple, spinach, cherries, and lemon in

a juicer and process until juiced. Transfer to a serving glass and stir in the water.

Add some crushed ice and serve immediately.

Nutrition information per serving: Kcal: 196, Protein: 9.2g, Carbs: 59.3g, Fats: 1.5g

50. Orange Apple Juice

Ingredients:

1 cup papaya, chopped

1 large orange, peeled

1 small Granny Smith's apple, cored

1 cup fresh mint, torn

1 tbsp fresh basil, torn

Preparation:

Peel the orange and divide into wedges. Cut each wedge in half and set aside.

Wash the apple and cut in half. Remove the core and cut into bite-sized pieces. Set aside.

Wash and peel the papaya. Cut lengthwise in half and scoop out the seeds. Cut into bite-sized pieces and fill the measuring cup. Reserve the rest in the refrigerator.

Rinse the mint and basil thoroughly under cold running water. Drain and torn into small pieces. Set aside.

Now, combine orange, apple, papaya, mint, and basil in a juicer and process until juiced. Transfer to a serving glass and add some ice.

Serve immediately.

Nutrition information per serving: Kcal: 199, Protein: 4.1g, Carbs: 60.1g, Fats: 1.1g

51. Parsnip Carrot Juice

Ingredients:

1 cup parsnip, sliced

1 large carrot, sliced

1 cup cauliflower, chopped

1 cup fennel, trimmed and chopped

1 whole lime, peeled

Preparation:

Wash and peel the parsnip. Cut into thin slices and fill the measuring cup. Reserve the rest for later.

Wash and peel the carrot. Cut into thin slices and set aside.

Wash the cauliflower and trim off the outer leaves. Cut into small pieces and fill the measuring cup. Reserve the rest for later.

Trim off the fennel stalks and outer wilted layers. Wash and chop the fennel into bite-sized pieces. Fill the measuring cup and reserve the rest for later. Set aside.

Peel the lime and cut lengthwise in half. Set aside.

Now, combine parsnip, carrot, cauliflower, fennel, and

lime in a juicer. Process until well juiced.

Transfer to a serving glass and refrigerate for 10 minutes before serving.

Add some turmeric or ginger for some extra taste. However, it's optional.

Nutrition information per serving: Kcal: 141, Protein: 5.6g, Carbs: 46.2g, Fats: 1.1g

52. Mint Apple Juice

Ingredients:

1 cup fresh mint, torn

1 large red apple, cored

1 cup blueberries

1 large cucumber, sliced

2 oz coconut water

Preparation:

Wash the mint thoroughly and torn with hands. Set aside.

Wash the apple and cut in half. Remove the core and cut into bite-sized pieces. Set aside.

Place the blueberries in a colander and wash under cold running water. Drain and set aside.

Wash the cucumber and gently peel it. Cut into thin slices and set aside.

Now, combine mint, apple, blueberries, and cucumber in a juicer. Process until juiced and transfer to serving glasses. Stir in the coconut water and refrigerate for 10 minutes, or add some ice before serving.

Enjoy!

Nutritional information per serving: Kcal: 258, Protein: 4.7g, Carbs: 74.6g, Fats: 1.6g

53. Brussels Sprout Pepper Juice

Ingredients:

1 cup of Brussels sprouts, halved

1 large yellow bell pepper, chopped

1 medium-sized fennel bulb, chopped

1 large cucumber, sliced

¼ tsp salt

2 oz water

Preparation:

Trim off the outer leaves and wash the Brussels sprouts. Cut in half and set aside.

Wash the bell pepper and cut lengthwise in half. Remove the seeds and chop into small pieces. Set aside.

Trim off the fennel stalks and wilted outer layers. Cut into bite-sized pieces and set aside.

Wash the cucumber and cut into thin slices. Set aside.

Now, combine Brussels sprouts, bell peppers, fennel, and cucumber in a juicer. Process until well juiced and stir in the salt and water. Refrigerate for 10 minutes before serving.

Nutritional information per serving: Kcal: 151, Protein: 9.7g, Carbs: 47.6g, Fats: 1.4g

54. Bean Beet Juice

Ingredients:

1 cup green beans, chopped

1 cup beet greens, torn

1 cup fresh mint, torn

2 cups celery, chopped

1 large cucumber, sliced

2 oz water

¼ tsp salt

Preparation:

Wash the green beans and cut into bite-sized pieces. Set aside.

Combine beet greens and mint in a colander. Wash under cold running water and torn with hands. Set aside.

Wash the celery and cut into small pieces. Set aside.

Wash the cucumber and cut into thin slices. Set aside.

Now, combine green beans, beet greens, celery, mint, and cucumber in a juicer. Process until well juiced and transfer to serving glasses. Stir in the water and salt.

Refrigerate for 10 minutes before serving.

Nutritional information per serving: Kcal: 91, Protein: 6.1g, Carbs: 26.1g, Fats: 1g

55. Lemon Swiss Chard Juice

Ingredients:

1 large lemon, peeled

1 cup Swiss chard, chopped

1 cup fresh basil, chopped

1 large Zestar apple, cored

1 cup fresh mint, chopped

2 oz water

Preparation:

Peel the lemon and cut lengthwise in half.

Combine Swiss chard, basil, and mint in a large colander. Wash thoroughly under cold running water. Chop into small pieces and set aside.

Wash the apple and cut in half. Remove the core and cut into bite-sized pieces. Set aside.

Now, combine lemon, Swiss chard, basil, mint, and apple in a juicer and process until well juiced. Transfer to serving glasses and stir in the water.

Refrigerate for 15 minutes before serving.

Enjoy!

Nutritional information per serving: Kcal: 126, Protein: 3.9g, Carbs: 39.1g, Fats: 1.1g

56. Tomato Cucumber Juice

Ingredients:

1 large tomato, chopped

1 large cucumber, sliced

2 cups beets, trimmed

3 large radishes, trimmed

½ tsp fresh rosemary, chopped

¼ tsp sea salt

1 oz water

Preparation:

Wash the tomato and place it in a bowl. Cut into bite-sized pieces and reserve the tomato juice while cutting. Set aside.

Wash the cucumber and cut into thin slices. Set aside.

Wash the beets and trim off the green parts. Cut into small pieces and set aside.

Wash the radishes and trim off the green ends. Cut in half and set aside.

Now, combine tomato, cucumber, beet radishes, and rosemary in a juicer. Process until well juiced and transfer to serving glasses. Stir in the salt and water. Refrigerate for 15 minutes before serving.

Enjoy!

Nutritional information per serving: Kcal: 152, Protein: 8.2g, Carbs: 44.9g, Fats: 1.2g

ADDITIONAL TITLES FROM THIS AUTHOR

70 Effective Meal Recipes to Prevent and Solve Being Overweight: Burn Fat Fast by Using Proper Dieting and Smart Nutrition

By

Joe Correa CSN

48 Acne Solving Meal Recipes: The Fast and Natural Path to Fixing Your Acne Problems in Less Than 10 Days!

By

Joe Correa CSN

41 Alzheimer's Preventing Meal Recipes: Reduce or Eliminate Your Alzheimer's Condition in 30 Days or Less!

By

Joe Correa CSN

70 Effective Breast Cancer Meal Recipes: Prevent and Fight Breast Cancer with Smart Nutrition and Powerful Foods

By

Joe Correa CSN

www.ingramcontent.com/pod-product-compliance
Lightning Source LLC
Chambersburg PA
CBHW030330080526
44584CB00012B/794